The Creative Christian Home

The CREATIVE Christian Home

Merla Jean Sparks

BAKER BOOK HOUSE
Grand Rapids, Michigan

ISBN: 0-8010-8050-9

Contents

Foreword

Merla Sparks comes honestly by her gift for writing in the Christian vein. Her heritage embraces, in addition to a godly home, a mother who for many years wrote for youth publications. Her own training includes a B.S. in English from the University of Cincinnati. And she writes, not from theory, but from her own experience as a mother of two: David, now 12; and 5-year-old Angela.

Mrs. Sparks's background experience was broadened by the two years she and her husband, Earl, spent as "occupational missionaries" in Australia, where Earl taught science and Merla wrote, looked after her husband, son, and homemaking chores, and bore Angela.

Her articles, including most of these chapters, have appeared in a number of religious and children's publications. This book will be welcomed for its down-to-earth practicality and for author Sparks's warm, open style.

—ROBERT W. MCINTYRE
General Superintendent, The Wesleyan Church

Preface

This book is not an authoritative text on child psychology—although I have strived to base all material on sound psychological principles.

Nor is this book a complete how-to manual that will give the Christian parent infallible guidance—although I have tried to carefully follow basic Christian principles.

This book has no "answers"—only "ideas." These ideas are not applicable to all children, at all ages, under all circumstances. To be candid, right now as I reread the manuscript just before it goes to the publisher, I am fully aware that not all the ideas are presently usable even within my own family.

Does that sound strange? Let me explain. I wrote and rewrote the material in this book over a period of five years —from the situation of one son, age 7, to the situation of one son, 12, and one daughter, 5. Each "idea" worked at one time, with one child. One might work many times with either child—some "ideas" wouldn't work the second time, even with the same child.

My hope is that you will consider this book only as a resource. Try anything that seems workable; modify anything that has some potential; disregard anything that doesn't seem practical in your home.

If by reading this book you are inspired to make your Christian home more creative—*whatever* that means to you—then the book will have achieved its purpose.

—MERLA JEAN SPARKS

Chapter 1

Your Child and . . .
His Individuality

My three-year-old David had shattered the quiet of the doctor's waiting room. He had fired one question after another in his shrill little voice, laughed noisily at the funny picture books, and stumbled over tables and chairs as he explored every corner of the room. I was exhausted from my efforts to hold him in rein.

Next to us was the only other child in the room, a pretty little girl about David's age, with round, sober eyes. The contrast was striking; for all during the long wait, she sat almost motionless on her mother's lap.

After setting up a lamp that David had toppled over, I turned to the other mother and commented enviously, "I wish David would sit quietly like your little girl."

I'll never forget the look of pain that flashed through her eyes, or her sad answer, "My baby has brain damage; she will never be able to run or talk or laugh like yours."

I've been a better mother since then, for that day I learned an important lesson. *We must accept our children as they are.*

Before I married, I had a highly romantic picture of

11

the ideal family: dainty, genteel little girls and handsome little gentlemen. But when my first never-still, fireball son arrived, my idealism floundered in the sea of reality. For three years I was frustrated, trying to reconcile David's boundless energy with my airy dreams.

Then came that illuminating incident in the doctor's office. I went home, subdued and thoughtful. Yes, it was selfishness that prompted my fantasies. I was not thinking about David's well-being, but of my girlhood dreams.

The scripture verse came to me, "Lo, children are an heritage of the Lord" (Ps. 127:3). When God gives a gift, His is an all-wise selection. Although our duty as parents is to mold and influence these lives God entrusts to our care, we must accept the basic materials we are given.

ACCEPTING THE PHYSICAL

How happy we are when the doctor announces, "You have a perfectly formed, healthy baby"! What mother hasn't given a happy sigh when the nurse unwrapped the baby for the first time and she could count each little finger and toe and with gentle fingers outline the lovely features on that sleeping face? Or how thankful we have been to see our children grow up to run with strong legs and play hard with healthy bodies!

When all is normal, it is not hard to accept our child's physical makeup. But when the doctor must announce that all is not well with the baby, or that "your child will never walk again," then heartache makes it harder for acceptance to come. Many heartbroken parents have had to cling during this time to Rom. 8:28: "All things work together for good to them that love God."

No matter how serious the limitations of a child, most parents of the physically handicapped agree that the sooner the family accepts the situation, the better for both the child and his parents. Ridding themselves of a negative emphasis will allow for positive adjustment.

Wise parents will not only resign themselves to the child's limitation, but will strive to offset it by emphasizing other factors. A child who is not athletic may excel in scholastic competition. A long illness that keeps a student out of school may present the opportunity to develop a new skill such as painting.

It is important that the parent does not yield to the ever present temptation to "baby" the handicapped child. He must be helped to avoid self-pity and, even more so than the average child, to develop independence. All of us can recall examples of radiant, cheerful people who have camouflaged the worst physical blemishes.

ACCEPTING THE MENTAL

Although physical handicap is difficult to accept, a mental retardation or abnormality in a child is one of the most crushing blows a parent can suffer. Platitudes by those who have not faced this are out of place here, and yet many families with this sorrow have been able to find unfaltering acceptance of God's plan for their lives and their child's.

A less dramatic but far more common problem in the area of mental development is the unrealistic goals parents set for children of average intelligence. With today's emphasis on better education, the conscientious parent wants his children to have every advantage.

However, a few guidelines can help him to encourage his child's mental growth and give vocational guidance without making unreasonable demands:

1. Realize and accept capabilities and limitations.
2. Respect individual differences.

13

3. Resist the urge to pressure into any educational or vocational choice.

4. Teach self-discipline, an asset in any occupation.

ACCEPTING THE EMOTIONAL

The placid, even-tempered, easy-to-discipline child is a parent's dream. But he rarely exists in real life. A child can be bossy, hyperactive, sullen, talkative, restless, selfish, overbearing, fidgety, jealous. In short, he is very human, with all the limitations that that implies.

As in the physical and mental areas of human development, there may be emotional abnormalities which demand professional care. But it is with the average child, with his normal range of emotional expression, that a parent is most likely to attempt a complete "overhaul." Although he accepts the boundaries of physical and mental capabilities, a parent may try to reshape completely a child's emotional makeup.

There is no area where individual differences are so evident as in the emotions. The same hereditary factors and an unchanging home environment still produce an infinite variety of personalities in one family.

The wise parent knows that his job is to channel rather than to change. The self-assertive child should be encouraged to be independent; he may thus develop the initiative that will make him a successful businessman. The bossy child should be given the opportunity to develop his leadership skills. The indefatigable dynamo, like my David, can be directed into creative activities where his unlimited energy is an asset, not a liability.

Some traits may not show their true worth until long past childhood. Take, for example, the sensitive child who becomes a compassionate social worker; the talkative one who becomes a successful salesman; the daydreamer who

14

writes or paints; the moody, restless one who becomes a scientist or an explorer.

GOD'S GIFT

"Every good gift and every perfect gift is from above, and cometh down from the Father" (Jas. 1:17).

We parents can accept our most priceless gift, our children, with thankful hearts—and accept them *just as they are*. For whatever God gives is perfect. Perhaps it is not perfect according to human standards, but it is perfect in God's plan for our particular family.

THE PARADOX OF PARENTHOOD

The idea of this whole chapter, you may now say, seems to preclude the need for any more chapters in this book. If we must accept our children as they are, why read a book that gives suggestions on how we can be better parents?

This does seem a paradox—but perhaps being a parent is one of the most paradoxical roles we have in life. We are always influencing our children with our own ideas, and yet encouraging them to be themselves at the same time.

This is not an unsolvable conflict, but a desirable balance. While we must firmly believe in the individuality of our children and accept each for his unique makeup—physical, mental, and emotional—we, as Christian parents, must fulfill our biblical roles as primary guides.

These next chapters are an effort to help you in this all-important job.

Chapter 2

Your Child and . . .
Discipline

If some book could be published which had all the answers, raising children could be the easiest task in the world. But your home library could not contain all the material written on child behavior and discipline. They run the gamut from the scholarly tomes of the professional theorists to the chatty paperbacks of "practical" mothers. But to compound the problem, all authors do not agree, and there is no such thing as an "average" child. In no area is the disparity more pronounced than in the matter of discipline. Should we throw up our hands in despair, pitch out the child-care books, and blindly grope our way, guided only by our own changing emotions and hazy personal theories?

Let's not be disturbed by this myriad of advice. It could be a *desirable* situation. In the area of child discipline, ignorance is not bliss. We must be aware of the *various alternatives* we have in dealing with our children. Only then can we intelligently choose the methods and ideas that will work best for our particular family.

The parents' personalities, the child's makeup, the home environment—all these are so varying that no one theory of child psychology can be said to be "absolutely right."

Therefore, we need to read widely on this subject. Although many secular authors will give reliable advice, it is well also to consult authorities that give a Christian emphasis to their psychology. A Christian bookstore usually has several inexpensive paperbacks on child rearing that would be helpful in every home.

I am giving the following example and comments as a small contribution to the store of advice on child discipline. It is not an overall view, but only one concept. However, it has been a very useful concept for me, giving direction many times when my emotions might have led me hastily and unwisely. My hope is that others might find it helpful too.

A CASE STUDY IN DISCIPLINE

Three-year-old Susie Bell was bent on "helping" her mother. She would fix Daddy's morning coffee.

She pulled the chair up to the cupboard and got down the coffee jar. My, wasn't Mommie going to be proud of her! She found the sugar bowl and carried it over to the table.

Crash!

Oh-h-h, dear . . . she had set it too near the edge and it had toppled off.

Just then Mrs. Bell arrived. "O Susie! Look what you've done this time. I'll have that gritty stuff under my feet for days." Jerking Susie into the living room, she smacked her firmly on the bottom and set her in the corner. "You can stay there while the rest of us eat breakfast —and I spend half the morning cleaning up your mess!"

The day passed. That evening Mrs. Bell called Susie in from the yard for supper.

"I don't want any supper."

"You must come in just the same," replied Mrs. Bell.

"Well, I won't." Susie flipped her blond curls and marched off toward the front sidewalk.

17

Mrs. Bell turned back into the house and sighed wearily, "I do wish that Susie were not so stubborn."

Two small incidents at the Bell home. Mrs. Bell will hardly remember them even the next day. Therefore, she would probably be very shocked to learn that these two incidents, although small, indicate a serious flaw in her method of discipline, a flaw that may produce disturbing behavioral problems with Susie in later years.

What general guidelines to discipline did Mrs. Bell overlook?

1. *Evaluate on motive rather than results.* Although spilt sugar is definitely exasperating and entails a difficult cleanup job, the motive behind Susie's actions—her wanting to help—was admirable. Mrs. Bell was so quick to condemn that Susie had no time to explain her planned surprise. It will be no wonder that Susie will be inclined to balk when her mother, at some later date, wants her to help in the kitchen. Why risk another accident and a scolding?

On the other hand, Mrs. Bell ignored a basic action of disobedience later in the day—because it caused her no immediate inconvenience. She could send her husband out for Susie later. But this was a time when she should have taken definite corrective measures immediately, for Susie's behavior indicated a deliberate defiance of serious importance.

2. *Distinguish between disobedience and awkwardness.* Evaluate the situation to see whether a child's action is purposely transgressive or just the impulsiveness of youthful exuberance. Skinned knees from running, torn clothes from climbing, odorous messes from collecting, unyielding stains from experimenting—yes, all of these make lots of work for a mother. But they are the natural results of the growing-up process.

We must ask ourselves: Is it willful unruliness or just typical "kid noise"? Is this action of his wrong, or does it just "make me nervous"?

But we may say, "I've told him a hundred times not to run to school. He's bound to fall." Is it wrong to want to run when you are seven? Are clean dresses and trousers without holes life's crowning achievement?

3. *Establish priorities.* A child must learn many lessons, but there is a limit to how much he can absorb at one time. Therefore, it is important to decide where to lay the stress. If "making a mess" is as big a crime as telling a lie, the child will never learn that truthfulness is much more important in life than tidiness. We need to make clear by our emphasis the difference between "necessities" and "nonessentials."

4. *Differentiate between training and punishment.* Deliberate misconduct should be dealt with firmly. The severity of the punishment should match the long-term importance of the offense.

Careless or awkward habits, those "rough edges," can be improved or overcome only by patient effort over a long period of time, usually measured in years rather than days or months. It is not possible to force a child to be quiet, poised, or dexterous. Any efforts to do so will only increase clumsiness or hypertensive reactions.

But there are ways that we can provide strong, although sometimes subtle, guidance to help a child develop self-control. Positive action, whenever possible, is best to elicit desirable behavior in children.

—Use praise more than blame.
—Foresee problem areas and deal with them before conflict develops.
—Encourage rather than nag.
—Strive for fairness.

19

—Listen to explanations before drawing final conclusions.
—Be consistent, but not inflexible.
—Recognize the need for public agreement on discipline between the parents. Settle any differences in private.
—Avoid ridicule, sarcasm, and irony.
—Give explanations for decisions whenever possible, although instant obedience without explanation may sometimes be necessary and expected.
—Set definite, clear limits of behavior, avoiding detailed or arbitrary rules that confuse.
—Make absolute decisions slowly, especially during times of weariness or tension. Use "maybe" instead of "no," or "I'll think it over," or "Not today, but maybe later."
—Give reminders kindly and in a matter-of-fact tone. Shun "making a scene."
—Consider individual differences in children and make judgments accordingly.

When chastening is necessary, oral or corporal, make sure tempers are cooled and you are not hasty or purely emotional in your judgments.

A PERSONAL TEST

Here is a good test to check our guidelines:

We have been painting the bedroom. We have closed the door and forbidden *anyone* to go in. Six-year-old Johnny takes advantage of our being in the basement momentarily and quietly opens the door and goes in.

When we discover him, what is our reaction?

That he must be disciplined for disobeying?

Or would we use a sliding scale of punishment?

a. *No paint on him:* Relief and a reminder not to go in again.
b. *Paint on his hands:* A firm scolding while rubbing furiously with turpentine.
c. *Paint on his clothes:* An intense lecture *and* a hard spanking.
d. *The bucket of paint overturned:* A vehement tirade *and* a hard, hard spanking *and* sent to bed without supper.

Let's honestly grade ourselves!

Disciplining children is a difficult task. Being overly stern and strict will cause hardness and rebellion. On the other hand, an easygoing, lackadaisical approach may produce unruliness and irresponsibility.

God's guidance is needed in finding a sensible middle course; for even though a well-disciplined child makes it easier to have a peaceful home, this is not the primary goal. The spiritual import is that this discipline will make possible for him a richer, more useful Christian life.

Chapter 3

Your Child and . . .
Mealtime

A traditional picture of a closely knit, happy family is of a smiling brood gathered formally around a massive, feast-laden table. But perhaps that sort of dream situation is a bit out-of-date in this hurried, "grab a hamburger" era. The solemn, dignified dining room ruled by the ponderous table that could grow to almost unbelievable lengths is practically museum material. Now there are tiny, efficient kitchen nooks, restaurant-sleek counters and stools, and modern, gala patio sets.

Is this change in tastes bad? Of course not; styles have always been changing. But it is an indicator of the growing informality of our lives.

Although there is nothing basically wrong with this switch to the casual, it is a contributing cause to the breakdown in family solidarity. Anyone who picks up a current newspaper or magazine cannot escape the realization that today's complex, rushed world is seeing the frightening disintegration of the tight family structure that has proved to be the nation's strength down through the years.

We Christian parents should be concerned about this

trend and take strong measures to counteract it in our own homes. It is important to realize that the spiritual growth of the individual members has definite correlation with the unity of the family. A lack of fellowship and communication on the home level breeds misunderstanding between adults and children and makes regular Christian training impossible.

Therefore, mealtime, when most often the family is together, can be a rich opportunity to cement bonds of family communion, which will, in turn, nurture a fertile atmosphere for spiritual growth.

To establish a program of increased family loyalty, it is not necessary that radical measures be adopted to insure that at all three meals a day there is 100 percent family attendance. Varied individual schedules would make this impossible for many families. But a desirable plan would be for the whole family to be able to sit down together for at least one meal a day.

This may necessitate some adjustments. Mother may have to give up her wish for an early supper, even though it means doing dishes later in the evening than she prefers. Lazy, morning sleepers could sacrifice a half hour's sleep to join the rest of the family for breakfast. If because of necessary irregular schedules complete cooperation is not possible every day, then several times a week would be a second-best alternative.

However, the value of mealtimes even when only part of the family can be present should not be overlooked, for they can be utilized in special ways to give important individual attention. A child who comes home from school for lunch can blossom out under the special, undivided attention that is possible for an otherwise busy mother. A father and teen-ager who must eat an early breakfast alone can find that this is a good chance to share ideas that could never be discussed in the noisy atmosphere of a regular meal. Mother's peaceful meal alone with a pre-schooler gives a chance for him to share his small interests without competing with the grander exploits of older sisters and brothers. A quiet meal for Mom and Dad after young children have been put to bed can give an opportunity for much-needed communication.

But there is no substitute for the mealtime when the whole family is present. It may be noisy, but it is a high point of the day—when exciting events are recorded, ideas shared, and plans made.

The following suggestions can make family mealtime more enjoyable and profitable:

1. *Strive for an unhurried atmosphere.* Since this is primarily the result of a relaxed mental attitude, we can cultivate this even if time is limited.

2. *Allow no negative conversation.* Combat criticism, complaint, and argument. Take advantage of the time together to make necessary group decisions and plan positive family projects and activities. This is not the time to discuss individual problems or deal with frictions in specific areas of disagreement.

3. *Guard against one person monopolizing the conversation.* Bring out quieter members with directed questions. Guide the conversation so that the older children's exciting recitals of their activities do not swallow up the younger's "just as important to me" stories. It is specially important that we parents do not dominate the conversation.

4. *Encourage free discussion on a wide variety of subjects.* Avoid controversial items that lead to family quarrels.

5. *Delay disciplinary action in almost all cases until the meal is finished.* Nothing ruins a meal faster than parent-child confrontations. Avoid these by:

   a. Ignoring petty infractions. Many of these are a

result of childish awkwardness anyway, not of deliberate disobedience.

b. Delaying action whenever possible. For example, when a child deliberately misbehaves, instead of dealing with the problem right then, we might say nothing until the meal is over. If there is general family disagreement, we must stop the discussion and set a later time, after the meal, for it to be continued and the problem worked out.

c. Using quiet methods if misbehavior needs immediate attention. Send the child (or children) to another room, rather than give a public lecture. If we must deal personally with one child, take him to another room, so the rest of the family may continue the meal in comparative calm.

6. *Give training in table manners.* At the same time, we must not let this dominate the atmosphere. It has been hard for our family to hit a happy medium in this area. My interest in proper manners gave rise to a habit of nagging. But it was hard to keep quiet when the children's table manners seemed unbearable. We worked out the following compromise that works *most* of the time for us.

a. We discussed the problem outside of mealtime. This seemed to be "neutral" territory, and made it easier to keep cool.

b. We decided together on the basic table manners we would stress. My husband and I would not nag about small "deviations" if the basic rules were being followed.

c. We established that this was a "training" area, not a "punishment" one. Therefore, if we had to point out when the children were violating a basic rule, they were to remember we were only *reminding* them, not *blaming* them. Our part was to see that our tones conveyed this.

d. We agreed on a couple of signals so we wouldn't have to verbalize the matter too often, especially when there was company or we were eating out. Two fingers raised for the "peace" sign means to cut down the excessive talking. A raised index finger means to slow down the gobbling.

7. *Make the saying of grace a meaningful activity.* It helps if we use varied forms: singing, spontaneous prayers, memorized verses. A good custom, especially in families with young children, is to join hands during grace; this gives physical force to the idea of a spiritual bond (as well as keeping active little hands still). Rotate the responsibility of leading grace.

8. *Supplement the family worship program with the use of a promise box or a "verse of the day" right after grace.* This could be a springboard for stimulating discussion during the meal.

9. *Take advantage of any established mealtime routine to facilitate a regular family worship program.*

If mealtime in our homes is cheerful, animated, positive, and inspiring, then it will be an important influence in our children's spiritual life.

Chapter 4

Your Child and . . .
Family Worship

"Time for family worship."

Do these words bring sighs from around the house? Or suddenly remembered "necessary appointments" somewhere else? Or the onset of a creeping paralysis that attacks young legs?

Or does it seem impossible to find a time when the whole family is at home? Does the phone interrupt? Does it seem that even a busy church program becomes a competitor?

Then perhaps this time-honored family institution is ailing at our house and needs a tonic; or, worse still, is dead and needs drastic revival treatment. It is an undeniable fact that this complex, rushing modern age creates special problems and added pressures. But how can we, as Christian parents, combat these in order to establish a meaningful family altar?

1. *We must be convinced of the importance of family worship.* It is not only desirable, but absolutely essential. Parents must bear responsibility for their children's religious education and not leave it completely to the church. Busyness, rather than being an obstruction, should demonstrate the heightened need for quiet "islands of time"

when spiritual nurture and revitalization are available for the whole family.

2. *We must be willing to spend extra time and thought in planning and preparation.* A regular, inspiring family worship program never just accidentally "happens"; only persistent effort will make it succeed.

3. *We must establish some kind of schedule.* This seems to be the biggest problem. Many active, Christian families are so involved in church, school, and community activities that it is difficult to find a time when all are at home together. Some priorities will need to be set up. If we are just too busy, even with "good" activities, to adequately take care of our family's spiritual welfare, then the only answer is to cut out something of lesser importance.

After we have set up a regular schedule, consistent effort must be exerted to keep it. The importance of common interruptions must be evaluated and measures taken to meet them. A good rule may be to ignore the phone, for probably there is no emergency that can't wait a few minutes longer. Or, if that isn't possible, assign one person to take messages.

If we have a varied daily routine, make the schedule flexible, such as having worship after breakfast on some days, at bedtime on others.

If children's ages and activities are very widespread, two periods a day could be set aside, so that members of the family can always have opportunity for at least one. But we should strive for 100 percent participation at least several times a week.

It is said of man that "he does what he wants to do." Time available for family worship depends largely upon the parents' values. Notice how many times in the week the whole family is in front of the TV. Why is this easier to arrange than family worship?

4. *We must present a challenging program.* This will

28

go a long way toward solving even the problem of scheduling. If family worship were the most interesting activity of the day, everyone would make a special effort to cooperate.

Variety is the key here; nothing kills interest like routine. If the same predictable structure is followed day after day, it is no wonder that family worship becomes a boring duty rather than an anticipated pleasure.

The possibilities are endless; we must use our imagination. Any religious bookstore will provide a wealth of new materials and ideas that can be adapted to fit our children's ages and interests. Listed are some suggestions for the Bible-training part of the family altar, covering the range of interests and capabilities from the youngest toddler to the most sophisticated teen-ager.

AN IDEA LIST

1. Read Bible stories, either directly from the Bible or from simplified storybooks, and follow with a "Were You Listening?" quiz.

2. Read a chapter in the Bible "round-robin"—especially good training for beginning readers. Vary Bible reading by alternating the King James Version and some of the new translations. Or choose a Bible passage for group discussion, taking turns being the "expositor."

3. Read a chapter a day in an exciting missionary biography, juvenile Christian novel, or spiritual "classic."

4. Use a book of daily devotional readings or a devotional guide that includes scripture, anecdotes, and inspirational writings.

5. Have a quicky debate or panel discussion on a timely topic.

6. Play games to learn Bible facts. There are many books and games on the market, such as "Who Am I?" "Fill in the Missing Word," "Twenty Questions," "Bible

Baseball," etc. "Sword drills" (looking up verses) and "spelldowns" can be used. Quizzes of all kinds can be arranged, with individual or team competition. Here again, there are many books available at a Christian bookstore.

7. Set up memorization programs, using charts and blackboard. Individual or group projects such as making visual aids, or holding competition and contests, encourage the learning of selected psalms, the Ten Commandments, the names of the disciples, the books of the Bible, soul-winning verses, etc.

8. Include music. Play religious records and organize group singing. Memorize old hymns and new choruses. Have sacred "concerts," from the preschooler rhythm band of kettles and spoons pounding out "Onward, Christian Soldiers" to the polished piano-violin duet rendition of "The Holy City."

9. Give a chance for expression in unusual forms. Pass out drawing paper and have each person illustrate a selected Bible story. In pantomime or skit, act out dramatic religious scenes.

10. Conduct an intensive study project on one book of the Bible or on a topic such as "faith." Use a concordance. Or study a subject of general knowledge—church history, denominational doctrines, missions, the catechism.

11. Use a flannelgraph and take turns telling stories with pictures.

12. Have a general "Question Time," when anyone can bring up religious, moral, or ethical issues.

13. Assign individual members to conduct family worship and let them work up surprise programs.

PRAYER TIME SUGGESTIONS

Making the prayer time of the family altar fresh and meaningful is especially important, and here again variety is needed to keep this treasured activity from becoming mere form. Quality, not quantity, should be emphasized. Long, rambling prayers full of clichés should be avoided by the adults.

Specific praying should be encouraged, with no pre-occupation with lengthy or polished phrasing. A diversity in basic emotional makeup and moods should be recognized, and every member should not be expected to pray every time.

1. Write out simple sentence prayers for use during the early training years.

2. Encourage spontaneous prayers, giving help with ideas when needed and wanted.

3. Memorize the Lord's Prayer and other prayers from the Scriptures.

4. Read prayers by the saints of the past and present.

5. Pray round-robin, limiting to one or two sentences each. Or try conversational prayer.

6. Have an all-praise prayer time.

7. Make a family prayer list, encouraging the listing of personal and family requests as well as those for outside interests.

8. Take a complete missionary family for a prayer partner project, choosing one with children near the ages of your own.

9. Occasionally vary the time with a period of silent prayer and meditation.

10. Rotate assignment of prayer leader, who is responsible for bringing requests and planning procedure.

Family worship can be the high point of the day. Let's make it that at our house.

Chapter 5

Your Child and . . .

Leisure Time

The way a child spends his leisure time has a significant bearing on his spiritual life. Therefore, we will want to help him make wise recreational choices.

FAMILY RECREATION

Provide a lively family recreational program. "A family that plays together stays together" is probably true.

The possibilities are endless for a family of any size or of any age range. Have picnics and backyard barbecues. Plan visits to the zoo, the beach, or historical landmarks. Organize game tournaments, in anything from Uncle Wiggly to badminton.

Vacations spent together can be a highlight in your children's life, and camping trips are tailor-made for many Christian families. It is not so important what the activity is so long as the whole family can enjoy it together.

Besides the obvious benefits of a close family circle, there is an important side result. Children who are busy enjoying family activities will have less time for outside interests of questionable value, and thus many problems and conflicts can be avoided.

Peer Companionship

We need to recognize the need for companionship within the same age-group. Although family ties are very important, our children need contact with children their own age. Young children will want to play with neighborhood friends. Older children will want to join their schoolmates in extracurricular functions.

Many of these associations are legitimate and desirable and should be encouraged for their value in helping a child adjust to a social environment. But a child often needs guidance in this area. In the early years it is important to keep a careful watch over his playmates and guard against harmful associations.

As he grows older, it is essential to provide opportunities for Christian friendship to counteract the overwhelming, worldly influence of schoolmates. Sometimes extra effort may be required if there are few children and young people in your church. For example, exchange visits can be arranged with a church in a neighboring city, or we can join a church recreational program of a sister denomination.

If the age difference or interests in a family are widespread, it is often wise to invite a child's friend along on family outings and vacations.

Dealing with Undesirable Activities

We must plan substitutes for undesirable activities. Often recreational possibilities offered by the school and the community are unquestionably harmful or unsuitable for our children. In such cases along with our prohibitions we would be wise to provide replacements.

If the boy scout hike is planned for Sunday, Father might take his son and some of his friends for a hike on another day. If a daughter feels left out because her class plans a dance, Mother might help her give a party for her Christian friends on the same night.

The important thing is to suggest appealing alternatives, so that a child will be less likely to yearn after the forbidden. Not that there must be a specific substitution in every case. This would force the parents into slavish pressures. But generally the child should be kept so busy with interesting, worthwhile activities and have enough suitable friends that questionable activities and undesirable associates will not be a plaguing issue.

LEISURE READING

Providing an abundance of elevating material for leisure reading is important. Children are not naturally discriminating; they will usually read what is readily available, providing it is easy enough and interesting.

Therefore, without making a big issue out of it, we can control most of our young children's reading choices by merely providing an adequate amount of worthwhile material, including much religious literature. Although not excluding secular selections, we should choose the books carefully for high educational and moral value.

With older children, when problems with questionable reading material occur (crime comics, sensational novels, etc.), clear explanations should be given, stressing basic principles, not legalistic considerations. It is usually not wise to make an absolute ban against a whole category (for instance, comics), but teach careful selection on individual merits. Sometimes it is best on borderline choices to merely discuss the issues with the older child and then let him make the final decision. This is an area where we can encourage the development of personal convictions.

TELEVISION

"Television and children" is a controversial subject, even without religious considerations. Conflicting reports have recently been published about the influence of TV violence on children.

But until more research is done in this area, parents, and especially Christian parents, will want to follow the generally accepted principle that TV must be *regulated* purposefully and conscientiously.

There are two factors here: the type of programs watched and the amount of time spent in watching.

The first factor is the easier to assess. Thoughtful consideration should tell us what programs are harmful. It is usually obvious which ones depict violence, low moral standards, or have other undesirable features. To see that none of these things contaminate the home, it is necessary for us to maintain close supervision. The interests and ages of the children should be considered and their wishes consulted. But children are rarely discriminating in their TV choices. They are not aware of the harmful aspects. So a parent must exercise the final judgment on what TV programs are to be watched.

The second factor is harder to evaluate. It is difficult to determine just how much even good television our children should watch.

Perhaps a good way to decide would be to run a test for several weeks. Keep track of how much TV is watched each day. Then for several weeks limit TV time. Take note of the effect.

1. Does family conversation become more frequent?

2. Are the children out in the fresh air and sunlight more often?

3. Is it easier to find time for family worship?

4. Is more reading done?

5. Do we have more opportunity to give personal attention to our children?

6. Are there fewer family arguments?

7. Does the house seem more calm and peaceful?

8. Is more time given to school homework? Do grades improve?

9. Do the children show more initiative and enthusiasm for creative activities?

An honest appraisal of the family's viewing habits may show the need for new limits.

The best time to establish TV limits is when the children are very young. Then they will accept the pattern of "Our program is over; now we turn off the set and go outside and play awhile."

If there are older children and the custom has been for the TV to be on constantly, we will have to expect some conflict over the new limits. But if we explain our reasons and the children see that we mean to enforce the limits, they will gradually become used to the idea.

Children will cooperate more cheerfully if they are given some voice in the matter. If they are allowed to watch two hours of TV per day and there are four hours of suitable programming, we should let them choose their favorite programs.

Our limits will also be accepted more readily if they are flexible. Perhaps we could permit more TV on rainy or cold days when the kids can't go outside. Perhaps we might allow them to stay up later for an extra-special program.

Whatever we decide, never allow television to rob the family of spiritual vitality.

Let 1 Corinthians 10:31 be our guide in helping our children make good use of their leisure time: "Whatsoever ye do, do all to the glory of God."

Chapter 6

Your Child and . . .
School

Never has education occupied such an important place in society. Not only are professional educators pre-occupied with new methods and expanded programs, but parents are showing more concern that the educational needs of their children are met.

Christian parents are especially interested in this area, for the school will influence their children more than any other factor outside the home.

CHRISTIAN SCHOOLS VERSUS PUBLIC SCHOOLS

Sometimes there is no choice as to where to send our children to school; there are no Christian ones in our area to consider. But if there is a choice, we should study the matter carefully.

Public schools vary greatly, not only from state to state, but within the districts themselves, depending on community pressures and administration. Therefore, we should evaluate each school individually, investigating such things as the teaching of evolution, the emphasis placed on moral and religious values, the latitude given for personal convictions.

The private Christian school should be investigated just as thoroughly; for it is not, as some assume, automatically the better choice. Ask yourself these questions:

1. Is the educational standard high enough? Circumstances may change (such as a family move), and if there is not easy transfer to a public school, the child may suffer, not only academically, but emotionally.

2. Does it have a well-rounded program that does not encourage bigotry and narrow-mindedness? One of the weaknesses of many private religious schools is that, in their effort to emphasize the higher goals of a Christian life, they sometimes become involved in petty issues or take fanatical stands.

Although the Christian school's purpose, to give the students solid training in "right" concepts, is desirable, there is the danger of encouraging intolerance and an uncharitable attitude toward the "outside world."

3. Is it close enough that daily transportation does not cut out valuable time for the child to be under home influence? Or more important still, if it involves boarding away from home, are the advantages great enough to merit this deprival of a normal home environment?

After comparing the alternatives, a decision can be made only by considering the individual child. Some seem to thrive in a public school environment; others seem to need a Christian school.

If the child is of strong personality, successful in his schoolwork, and well adjusted with his peers, the public school can be a wise choice. This challenge of being in an environment that is not sympathetic to Christianity often brings out a strength of character that will prove valuable in later years, when a totally Christian environment is not available. These children may often be better able to stand anti-Christian pressures in later life.

On the other hand, if a child is shy and finds it diffi-

39

cult to mix in public, or has trouble academically, or is easily influenced by others, then the protective atmosphere of a Christian school, at least for some part of his education, might be the one thing that will help get him established before meeting the pressures of a totally secular environment.

However, it is wrong to expect the Christian school to be a cure-all. A rebellious child who is a problem in the public school will not necessarily respond favorably if he is transferred. There may be many other factors influencing his behavior that will cause just as much conflict, or even more, in a totally religious atmosphere.

BECOMING INVOLVED

We need to become involved in our child's school program. Joining the PTA or other parent organizations is one way. Usually more can be done to influence school policy by working within the framework of existing organizations than by taking matters to the administration individually.

In public meetings we can speak up against school policies we feel are detrimental to our children's welfare. Often we will have ample support from people who may be too reticent to bring up the matter but who are just as concerned as we are.

In all public stands, we must be sure our attitude is kind and Christlike. Opposing wrong does not necessitate a harsh and argumentative spirit. A forceful but calm and well-prepared one-minute speech will accomplish more than a 10-minute harangue.

A TEACHER'S AUTHORITY

A basic rule for parents is to always uphold the teacher's authority. This does not mean the child should be taught his teacher is always right—he'll find out very quickly this just isn't true. But he should be taught that the teacher is in charge of his own classroom. Ordinarily, a child should not expect the parent to interfere with the teacher's educational methods or disciplinary measures.

In many cases a child is embarrassed by a parent's intrusion and would rather settle any problems himself. A parent's overprotective attitude here robs the child of valuable training in independence.

When we do question things about our children's school life, there is a proper procedure to follow. We should use regularly scheduled teacher-parent conferences as much as possible. Many troublesome issues our children bring home will naturally disappear if we let them ride until the next conference.

In a conference, let the teacher discuss his ideas and feelings first. Often this will answer many of our questions. If not, let's be candid; ask what we want to know. Any good teacher is happy to have an interested parent.

If we feel there is a problem so serious that we must have a special conference with the teacher immediately —when basic convictions are being attacked and the child is unwilling or unable to settle the matter himself—then we should make an appointment. In most schools the proper procedure is to request this through the school office.

In such interviews, we need to be careful that our attitude is cooperative and nonvindictive. Don't assume the teacher is wrong; often children do not get their facts exactly straight. In almost all cases, a mutually agreeable arrangement can be worked out or a satisfactory compromise reached.

Only in the rare possibility of an impasse would it be necessary to take the issue to a higher level—to the principal or the school board. And that should be done only for very basic issues.

It is a rare teacher or administrator who will not respect high moral standards and personal religious convictions. When there has been trouble, it has usually been the result of a harsh, antagonistic, untactful approach by the child or parent.

Academic Progress

We should show an interest in the child's academic progress. Inspire him to do his best, but do not pressure him with goals that are beyond his interests or capabilities.

We must also encourage good study habits in the light of 2 Tim. 2:15: "Study to shew thyself approved unto God, a workman that needeth not to be ashamed."

Listen to Him

Being a ready listener to that "right after school" chatter is vitally important. Almost all young children come home from school anxious to share the details of their day. No matter how trivial or silly these sometimes seem, it is important to demonstrate genuine enthusiasm for this free flow of ideas. If this becomes an established custom in the early school years, the problem of blocked communication during the teen-age years may never develop.

Extracurricular School Activities

Advocate participation in worthwhile extracurricular school activities. Many well-meaning parents forbid any school activities except the bare scholastic requirements, thinking that in this way problems can be evaded. But this can be a dangerous policy, for the child may experience severe emotional disturbance because of this total estrangement from the common activities of his age-group.

A wiser course seems to be one of controlled choice. With most schools offering a wide variety in their extracurricular programs—music, sports, clubs, art, drama—there are many activities that can broaden and stimulate the interests of our children without violating any Christian principles. In fact, they will probably give that essential sense of belonging.

Many parents wisely encourage their children to seek active roles in extracurricular activities. The "be not conformed to this world" idea does not mean a hermitlike withdrawal. Many Christian students, holding leadership positions, have provided a strong, spiritual impact in their schools.

Each activity must be judged on its own merits. And, as with many decisions, family and individual priorities must be considered.

For those generally worthwhile programs that have an occasional questionable event, it is often a good Christian witness for the child to withdraw from that particular event without dropping the whole program. On the other hand, some activities have goals that are so primarily against Christian principles that the best course would be to avoid them entirely.

The school is a strong molder of our children. Let's work with it closely, so we can help it do the best possible job for us and our children.

Chapter 7

Your Child and . . .
The Church

The organized Church is under attack from every side.

The liberals taunt, "Why aren't you interested in social reform?"

Psychology accuses, "You aren't solving man's personal problems."

The hippie jeers, "Man, you just aren't with it."

Even from within, the theologian flaunts his heresy, "God is dead—and so is the Church."

Is the established Church a dying institution? Or can we, as Christian parents, be influential in encouraging its increased vitality in the next generation?

"I was glad when they said unto me, Let us go into the house of the Lord" (Ps. 122:1). How can we help make these words the true response of our children?

Church Attendance

First, we can show by example that the church is an important part of our own lives. We must establish the habit of regular attendance.

Do visitors consistently keep us away from the Sunday services? Does a frantic secular schedule make it impossible to cooperate with special revival efforts? Then perhaps it is time to sit down and assess our values and goals in life.

This is not to mean that we and our families must be in church every time the doors are open. This has become such a binding and overemphasized concept to some that they have become uncharitable, and their children have rebelled against unreasonable demands.

Families with young children may have to make special arrangements for church attendance. Some parents cope better than others with their children in church. Some children seem to find it more "natural" to sit quietly. Therefore, this question will have to be settled on an individual basis.

If we don't have any problem with our young children in church, by all means we should take them along every time. But if (as it is with the majority) this is a very real problem, here are some suggestions that may be helpful:

1. Work up gradually the length of time the child must sit quietly. Some families use daily family worship as a training time for proper church behavior.

2. Take into consideration special factors, such as hot weather or lack of sleep. Sometimes the sensible thing is to stay home.

I can remember times when I stayed home to put a tired, fussy two-year-old to bed rather than struggle during a Wednesday night prayer service. I felt more "religious" praying alone in my bedroom while the child was asleep upstairs.

3. Pack up a "church bag," full of soft toys and books, suitable for the age of the child.

I have three bags for my four-year-old Angela that I interchange periodically, so everything seems "new." Favorite items are a new box of fat crayons and coloring book and a "magic stick-on" set.

4. Consider having the husband and wife (or older child) take turns staying home if it seems unwise to take a younger child to every service.

5. Utilize the church nursery, toddler church, or kindergarten church when these are available. If the church doesn't have these, suggest that one be provided—at least for some of the services. There are other tired mothers who need the refreshing, spiritual uplift of uninterrupted worship.

6. Consider getting a baby-sitter so both parents can enjoy special services. Think of the "spiritual vacation" for a husband and wife to attend together every night of a week's Bible conference.

After children start school and become more self-disciplined, then it is easier to make church attendance a regular family activity. But the attitude of the parents needs to set the pattern here. Being enthusiastic about the services, looking forward to special programs, discussing interesting ideas in the sermons—all these help build up a child's interest in church attendance.

Children are not very impressed with the concept "You'll go to church every time we tell you to whether you like it or not." This is not to imply that we would let a child stay home every time he wants to. If everyone did that, there wouldn't be a 10-year-old boy in church.

But we should let a child express his feelings about church attendance, and should not make him feel guilty if those thoughts are negative.

"Yes, Brian, I know you hate long services; I get tired too."

"I know it's hard for you to sit still. I remember I was fidgety in church at your age."

Often this type of understanding discussion will relieve the tension and the child will actually find it easier to sit still. The worst thing we can do is relate a child's behavior in church to his "religion."

As my 10-year-old once put it so aptly, "Just because I can't sit still in church doesn't mean I don't love the Lord."

I'm afraid some parents are expecting more of their children than the Lord does!

I see no reason why an especially restless child, even one up to 11 or 12, might not be given some special "props" to help him through the service:

A pad of paper to write down things he hears the preacher say. And if he doodles a lot, that doesn't mean he isn't still getting a lot out of the service.

A small tape recorder. Perhaps he would later play the tape for a shut-in or send it to a friend or relative in the armed services.

A "keep your hands busy" item. Some children can sit more quietly and even listen better holding a ball of clay or a piece of string or two paper clips.

Some families, because of unusual circumstances, may find it best to stay home from church occasionally. One parsonage family used to never go out to church when they were on their camping vacation. The children, now grown, say their small family worship service around the campfire is one of their strongest memories of spiritual inspiration.

Another family I know sometimes stays home from church on Sunday evenings. The father is out of town much of the time, holding Christian leadership seminars. On the occasional weekend he is not involved in Christian service he feels that sometimes the important thing to do is spend a leisurely Sunday evening at home and give his special attention to his family. The special family worship time is doubly meaningful.

However, care must be taken that any obstruction to

47

regular church attendance be thoughtfully evaluated. Priorities must be considered. Secular and unnecessary activities must not overshadow. Children will sense the difference between reasons and excuses long before they can consciously distinguish between them.

RESPECT FOR GOD'S HOUSE AND HIS PEOPLE

Second, we must teach respect for the church.

This begins with early training of attitude to the building itself. From infancy children should be sensitive to the church as a special, honored place and taught that the sanctuary has sacred importance. This does not mean to demand unreasonable behavior control, but to encourage the growth of a reverent attitude.

Respect for the church, however, is more than demanding proper behavior in the building itself. For the church, in its broader and more important sense, is not merely a solemn, awesome structure, but a group of people. This is an area where respect must be cultivated, too.

"Brotherly love" is the biblical command, but a censorious spirit by us as parents will destroy any chance of developing this attitude in our children.

Probably more damage to the reputation of the Church, and therefore its effectiveness, is caused by careless, critical talk around the dinner tables of church families than results from all the blows of opposing theologians and an unsympathetic outside world. If harsh judgments are passed on fellow Christians, and church leaders are disparaged at every turn, then it is no wonder that children grow up with a flippant regard for the Church and its usefulness. Our children's high esteem for the office of the clergy can be expected only if a pattern of respect and deference has been set by us through the years.

48

Promoting Denominational Loyalty

Third, we must promote denominational loyalty. Our children need to be taught the history of the denomination and its basic doctrines. We ourselves should be familiar with its organization at all levels and promote family cooperation with its programs, such as helping to choose the children's missionary prayer partners, visiting open house at one of the church colleges, participating in district summer camps.

When our juniors show a growing interest in spiritual matters, we should begin to encourage church membership.

Avoiding Bigotry

Fourth, we must guard against the formation of bigoted attitudes. Although denominational loyalty is admirable, caution must be exercised that this does not lead our children into a narrow-minded uncharitableness. Positive teaching about our own beliefs need not produce negative attitudes toward differing ideas.

In the case of false cults and religions with major differences, specific teaching is necessary. This could make a very stimulating and helpful family worship study project, with much help on the subject in paperback and pamphlet form available at any Christian bookstore.

As with all teaching about negative ideas, though, an emphasis on positive, correct beliefs is the most successful technique to combat opposing ones. To strengthen this area of knowledge, perhaps we could suggest that our church start graded catechism classes, if they are not already offered.

Although a strong teaching program is needed to help children escape the trap of false religions, it is often in the

49

area of minor denominational differences that we find the most problems in fundamental Christian homes. Here are some "rules" to consider:

1. Guard against prejudice and pettiness.

2. Emphasize individual evaluation rather than broad, sweeping generalizations. Avoid labels, such as "a formal church" or "liberal theology"—expressions that are so ambiguous that they are meaningless anyway.

3. Keep an open mind on varying church standards and allow free discussion on differing ideas. (This is such a subtle area. Usually parents never come right out and say, "That person is not a Christian because he does such-and-such and we don't." But the implication is there.) Parents with very rigid standards often have a spiritual smugness that develops in their children a "better than thou" attitude.

4. Encourage children to have a self-disciplined, personal standard while retaining a tolerance for varying principles in others.

A word of warning is needed here. We must keep in mind that setting "family standards" does not automatically result in their becoming our children's "personal standards."

When our children are young, it is our responsibility to lead them in the path of our personal convictions. But as they become older and begin thinking more for themselves, we must accept the fact that they will have some differing ideas, including some about religious issues. There is the inescapable fact of individuality. We may demand that our children do or don't do certain things as long as they are in our home, but we can never force them to "believe" in these standards.

Wise parents will allow for a free expression of differing opinions in the home. We must have understanding when a child does not agree with some of our standards.

50

This is an age-old conflict. We dare not give harsh judgments. Nor should we feel that their voicing opposing ideas is a threat to our authority.

This does not mean we will allow our children complete freedom of choice. We have the right—even the duty—to establish "house rules" which a child must keep even if he disagrees with them. But we must be careful that we do not try to force *belief* in certain standards. If we do, we may find him struggling with guilt feelings when he must make his own decisions.

SUPPORTING CHURCH ACTIVITIES

Fifth, we must support and encourage church activities that meet the needs of specific age-groups. It is of vital importance to our children that they have Christian friends their own age.

As well as making it possible for them to participate in the regular local Sunday school and youth programs, we should give as many other opportunities for Christian fellowship as we can. This will include summer camps, retreats, rallies, vacation Bible schools, etc. If activities are limited in our own denominational structure, we can supplement with programs of other evangelical groups. In some cases, we may have to organize some activities on our own to provide for this need, such as a neighborhood Bible club, or a Christian teen-age club.

The church is one of God's vital means of grace; so let us give it the fullest opportunity to spiritually nurture our children.

Chapter 8

Your Child and . . .

Sabbath Observance

"I dread those long Sunday afternoons."

"Why can't we do this on Sunday?"

"Sunday is such a boring day for us kids!"

These oft heard comments point up one of the knottiest problems of the Christian family. What standards to set for Sabbath observance is a question that often sharply divides the adults and children into opposing camps.

But it is a problem that we cannot afford to ignore or treat lightly, for it is of great consequence how our children spend the Sabbath. A wise use of the time can provide a real boost to their spiritual growth. Unwise handling of this subject can encourage in them at least a spiritual carelessness or, in the extreme, a rebelliousness that will filter into other areas of religious attitudes.

Although the life of the Christian family is Christ-centered seven days a week, Sunday should be given special consideration.

A SACRED DAY

Sunday should be considered sacred. "Remember the sabbath day, to keep it holy."

Regular church attendance will provide the best basis

to promote this, and our children should expect to go to church every Sunday if illness or special circumstances do not hinder.

But there are additional ways to keep this day holy. These may vary from family to family, depending on personal convictions and denominational customs. I have listed here some of the ways people use to help remind them that Sunday is a sacred day.

1. Abstaining from unnecessary business matters. The housewife will plan her needs ahead, so she doesn't have to buy groceries on Sunday. The insurance or real-estate man will not make a Sunday appointment. Children will not expect to stop at the Dairy Queen on Sunday—although in hot weather a wise mom will probably see that there is ice cream in the freezer when the family gets home!

2. Avoiding needless work. Dad mows the lawn on Saturday, rather than Sunday. Mom doesn't decide Sunday is a good day for everyone to clean out the basement.

3. Reading Christian literature, playing Bible games, and listening to religious records.

A MEANINGFUL DAY

The spirit of the law, rather than the letter, should be accented to make Sunday meaningful. If glorifying God is the decided aim rather than keeping a set of arbitrary, difficult rules, your children will be much more likely to see the reason for careful Sabbath observance and cooperate with a willing spirit.

For example, on a family camping trip when the customary church attendance may not be possible, a family campfire service may leave a more lasting impression than any standard means of worship.

One way to make Sunday more meaningful is to discuss the subject with the whole family. This discussion should bring out the basic principles involved. When children understand these, then specific do's and don'ts make a lot more sense.

Find out their ideas of Sabbath observance. They may make distinctions you never thought of. Two Sunday "rules" that a child decides upon for himself are worth more than 20 parent-made ones.

A DISTINCTIVE DAY

Sunday should be distinctive. Its plan of activities, with the emphasis on the spiritual, should set this day apart from the secular routine during the rest of the week. But stressing this aspect does not require exclusive preoccupation with religious pursuits. Such a legalistic aim is usually very difficult to achieve and can produce a rebellious attitude in children.

A more realistic position is to avoid a detailed, rigid standard and concentrate on achieving a more general identification with the spiritual. Therefore, there is room for individual judgment by each family.

I know of a home where the children decided that, since they ride their bicycles all week long, they would put them away on Sunday to show that this was a special day. On the other hand, another household with a very busy schedule all week may find that a Sunday afternoon, all-family bicycle ride might be just the right thing for them.

It probably does not matter so much about the details, but it is important that some differentiation be made that tags the day, "Reserved for God."

A REASONABLE DAY

Sunday regulations should be reasonable. Children, constantly active for six days, cannot be expected to suddenly stop dead still on the seventh and tranquilly sit and do nothing all day. We must take into consideration the child's natural makeup.

An adult's desire for a long Sunday afternoon nap is not usually present in a child. Neither is it likely that he finds it easy to spend all day on exclusively religious thoughts and activities; his spiritual maturity is not developed enough for this.

It is disturbing to hear a parent say, "Don't be so noisy; it's Sunday." Or, "We don't run and play rough on Sunday."

What does an active seven-year-old think when he hears this sort of thing? "God must like only big people; little kids must make Him nervous because we're so noisy!"

Although we might suggest less robust play on Sunday, we are wise to make allowance for a child's physical and mental limitations and plan the Sunday program accordingly.

A RESTFUL DAY

Sunday should be restful. This rest should not be interpreted as complete inactivity or synonymous with the "Sunday afternoon nap." God's rest on the seventh day was a cessation from the duties of creation; man's rest should be a change from the workday routine, a halt in its regular duties and responsibilities.

Physical rest is sometimes desirable for our children, but a mental rest which comes from a change in routine is even more necessary. Medical authorities strongly support this principle which God knew was necessary in order for man to have good physical and mental health.

Of course, some may take this as license for a completely secular program of recreation for Sunday, but any family that does is ignoring the other guidelines.

This restful characteristic is reason for many do's and don'ts that are not easily decided by other criteria.

For instance, should you allow your children to do school homework on Sunday? In itself study is a proper and necessary activity. But could it be done on Friday night or Saturday, so that Sunday could be free from the normal pressures of education? You must decide that in the light of your own family's situation.

My son likes to save his homework for Sunday. He does not feel it is a pressure, but a suitable quiet occupation as a change from his usual superactive pace. Others will as strongly assert that school is the child's "work" during the week, so to do schoolwork on Sunday is wrong. For example, my husband, working on his master's degree, felt that study was a demanding concern of his for six days; therefore, he needed Sunday for a complete rest of mind.

What about watching TV on Sunday? There are often inspiring religious and educational programs that could add to the day's meaning. Perhaps this is the one time during the week that the family can get together and enjoy a favorite program.

But if the clamor of TV dominates the home atmosphere all week long, perhaps it might be more quieting to banish this outside intrusion for the day.

AN INTERESTING DAY

Sunday should be interesting. It should be the highlight of the week, a day to anticipate, not to dread.

Without violating any of the first five principles, we can, with a little effort and foresight, make Sunday a day of delight, rather than boredom. Here are some summary ideas which might help.

1. Plan a varied program. Anything, no matter how exciting, dulls with over-repetition.

2. Alternate active and quiet activities. For instance, suggest a vigorous walk after a long church service.

3. Emphasize family activities. Often Sunday is the only day when the whole family has leisure time together; so a drive, or a popcorn feast, or Bible games, or a musical jam session might be your family's special interest.

4. Provide opportunities for Christian fellowship. Invite a family of similar interests to share your day. Encourage your children to participate in church-sponsored Sunday programs—youth groups, visitation, rallies. Arrange exchange of visits between your children and their Christian friends.

5. Suggest worthwhile projects. They might make scrapbooks for children's hospitals, or entertain shut-ins with a tape recording of the morning worship service, or baby-sit for a tired neighbor while she has a needed rest.

Strive to make Sunday in your home the very best day of the week.

Chapter 9

Your Child and . . .
Stewardship

"The best things in life are free" sounds good on paper, but in everyday life it would be hard to prove it! The fact is that financial matters take up a great deal of our time and attention. And since this is an inescapable problem in the life of every family, it is a good place to emphasize Christian attitudes and actions.

It cannot be stressed too heavily that the parents' example in this area, more so perhaps than in any other, is much more influential than are any training techniques that may be used. If the parents live only for material gain and practice a self-centered, grasping kind of existence, then any effort to promote generosity of spirit in their children would be in vain.

Before denials of this sin are made, let's look at some of those attitudes that creep into even the most respected church homes. A carelessness in tithing, or a quibbling over "net versus gross" tithable income; a second job, or mother working, just to provide the luxuries of modern society, with no regard for the needs of the family; a family egoism that leaves no time for entertaining the evangelist during a revival, or inviting the pastor's family home for

Sunday dinner; an indifference to missionary needs; the refusal to "ruin" the new car's beautiful upholstery just to pick up some rowdy Sunday school pupils; a self-righteous withdrawal from the needy members of the community —all are symptoms of this kind of materialism.

TEACHING THRIFTINESS

Thrift is a virtue that seems to suffer in America's prosperous atmosphere. "Wasting" money doesn't seem so important when there is always plenty more.

However, a Christian philosophy would not allow a slackness in handling finances. Every dollar that is wasted in unwise or unnecessary spending would be a dollar that could have been given for the Lord's work. Therefore, Christian stewardship must be based on sound financial principles.

One of the best ways to teach our children thriftiness is to give them regular allowances, gradually increasing the amount according to age, needs, and the financial responsibility shown. It will be necessary to specify what the amount should cover—whether it is just for childhood "luxuries" or must cover clothes, school expenses, lunches, general spending money.

But after those general guidelines, the child should be allowed to make his own decisions—and his own mistakes! The most we can do is give reliable information on alternative options (for example, this toy can be bought cheaper at the store up the street, or the quality of this is better than that).

The lessons the child learns best are in those experiences where he makes his own decisions, and sometimes unwise choices teach the strongest lessons of all.

We should resist the temptation to show an "I told you so" attitude. The child will more likely come to us for advice in the future if we have been understanding of his past mistakes in judgment.

On the other hand, we shouldn't "bail out" the child who has squandered his allowance early in the week. An advance (not a gift) might be needed on occasion for necessary expenses. Or we might give the opportunity for the child to *earn* some extra money. But the goal is to teach how to live within a budget. This means that the child must take the inevitable results of overspending—that is, doing without for a time.

CHRISTIAN STEWARDSHIP

If our attitudes about material things are in focus with a Christ-centered life, and we have taught our children basic financial responsibility, we have a good foundation for teaching Christian stewardship.

1. Teach tithing. Make that first allowance 10 pennies. Then the concept of tithing can be understood by even a very young child—1 penny out of every 10 is the Lord's. As the child gets older, raise the allowance only in multiples of 10 until a mathematical understanding of fractions is clear.

Extend this training on tithing to include all money received by the child, such as gifts or extra earnings. After several years we will find that tithing is an integral part of the child's life and will probably remain a routine, lifelong habit with little emphasis necessary at a later age.

2. Encourage generous giving. Although the habit of putting the tithe into a regular place should be established (perhaps in the Sunday school when the child is young and in the church when he is older), extra giving above tithe should be encouraged. Missionary appeals and special offerings have "built-in" attraction, so there is usually no problem in promoting these. Force should not be used,

of course, but children are usually eager to give. This is the place where enthusiasm and example by the parents play an important role.

A problem sometimes arises when an overzealous giver makes an unrealistic pledge. Extra chores may give the child a chance to earn the needed amount. However, even if the child has to make painful sacrifices, it is best for the parent to avoid outright "help." To do so robs the child of a valuable lesson in independence. At the same time we must do nothing either to turn him off on pledging or to take a careless attitude toward a pledge once it is made.

3. Suggest ways to earn money for special projects. Pay younger children for extra household jobs that are beyond their regular family chores, such as sweeping the sidewalks, or scrubbing the floor, when they want to earn extra money for a missionary project. When the youth club is raising money to go to camp, help older children find odd jobs around the neighborhood, cleaning out garages, mowing lawns, or baby-sitting.

4. Organize family-giving programs. Have a piggy bank on the dinner table and see how fast the family can reach a predetermined goal on a specific missionary project. Agree to limit family Christmas gifts and pool the rest of the money to help someone in need. Or spend part of the family vacation in helping to redecorate the church.

5. Emphasize self-denial. Example and suggestion are the only suitable methods here. Force, and especially too much mental pressure, is harmful. Total family involvement can be encouraged in this area by enthusiastically promoting local and denominational stewardship.

Suggest a variety of ideas from which members of the family could choose, adjusting this to the ages of the children. Giving up one ice-cream cone may be as meaningful to a five-year-old boy as the delay of a new dress may be to the 10-year-old daughter. Suggest cooperative family plans occasionally—like giving up supper desserts for one week in order to make a special offering to the church building fund.

No, money *isn't* everything, but a family that lives unselfishly devoted to the service of others will achieve a happiness that *is* worth everything.

Chapter 10

Your Child and . . .
Virtuous Living

Respect for elders, patriotic loyalty, industriousness, temperance, mannerliness—these used to be standard virtues taught in almost every American home. Parents did not have to be Christians to expect obedience, purity, and honesty in their children.

But for many people today these virtues are considered old-fashioned. Patriotism is out—civil disobedience is in. Virginity is out—the "new morality" is in. Self-discipline is out—the permissive psychology of situation ethics is in. Absolute truth is out—expediency is in. An honest day's work is out—getting something for nothing is in.

Should we, as Christian parents, feel liberated from the rigid code of the past and embrace this new social freedom? Or, on the other hand, should we become rabid champions of reform and advocate a return to the "good old days"?

As with all extremes, neither of these attitudes is desirable. But what is desperately needed is a solid, Bible-based training program in the Christian home to raise the moral tone on the family level. This will, in turn, have an uplifting effect upon the social standards of community and nation.

The best way to encourage moral excellence in our children is, first, to teach all values in the light of scriptural advice. "God says this is the right way" is stronger than "We don't allow this." But explanations should be made why God included specific do's and don'ts. The Ten Commandments should not be given as mere rote to memorize and blindly follow. We should warn our children about the results of breaking these rules—the confusion, the guilt, the unhappiness. The New Testament teaching on the spirit of the law, rather than the letter, should be emphasized.

Second, we should be positive in our approach. almost every "thou shalt not" has a more challenging "but do this instead."

Third, we should be shining examples of what we advocate. What our children see in us has an overpowering influence upon them. It begins "teaching" long before we verbalize precepts, and it always "outshouts" anything we say.

HONESTY

Lying and stealing are included in several biblical lists of basic sins. And even in this age of declining morals, most would condemn an outright untruth or theft. But the danger for our children is in the current philosophy that condones the gray zone of the half-truth; the dim, undelineated realm of the "accepted" cheat. Examples of this are incomplete listing of one's income on his tax returns, keeping a dollar mistakenly given in change, phoning long distance and asking for a prearranged absentee, using a friend's nontransferable discount card, breaking the speed limit. Only if absolute honesty is practiced in the home can this be the standard expected in our children.

Special attention should be given to scholastic ethics. Cheating is so prevalent in school that, unless a child is forewarned, it can become an accepted habit. He should be taught the fallacy of rationalizing that "everyone is doing it."

Excessive pressuring for good grades should be avoided, since this tends to push children into cheating practices. It is better to give strong praise for their best efforts, for this helps develop a sense of personal achievement that does not depend on public recognition.

PURITY

The movie industry makes immorality its biggest drawing card. Advertisements, subtly or patently, are built around sex appeal. Books make the best-seller lists by their lust-filled pages. Even many churchmen applaud the "new morality."

But despite society's encouragement of unrestricted sexual freedom, it has provided no answers to the guilt and shame which result.

The Bible truths have never been disproved: "The wages of sin is death." "Whatsoever a man soweth, that shall he also reap."

Therefore, our children must be shown that the glamor of the sensual life eventually fades into remorse and heartbreak, and the purity of mind and body is one of the most necessary virtues for a happy life.

OBEDIENCE TO PARENTS

The Bible gives special emphasis to this by making the fourth of the Ten Commandments the only one with promise.

In any home, the loss of parental authority spells disaster, but particularly in the Christian one; for when the children lose respect for their parents, little religious training can be accomplished. And more seriously, a child who has never learned to obey his parents will find it very difficult to surrender his will to God and give Him absolute obedience.

TEMPERANCE

With advertising such a powerful force in today's culture, it is more important than ever to warn children and teach them about the degrading influence of alcohol, tobacco, and harmful drugs.

To counteract the aura of glamor and prestige that advertising gives smoking and drinking, definite teaching should be given about their dangerous effect on physical and mental health. "Your body is the temple of the Holy Ghost."

Temperance, however, is more than abstinence from harmful habits; it is self-control in all areas of life. Paul speaks of this in 1 Cor. 9:24-27 when he compares the Christian to the disciplined athlete in a race. This attitude of moderation is one of the most priceless assets we can help our children develop, for it will open to them a wide variety of opportunities for Christian service.

Self-discipline means economy in financial matters— not being wasteful or extravagant. It means being content in the midst of unalterable circumstances, and not chafing or being envious of others. It means simplicity of desires, not being grasping and materialistic.

PATRIOTISM

Although scorned by many people today, a patriotic spirit is becoming to a Christian. Children should not see

66

just the sentimental, superficial meaning of this attribute, however, but rather its practical application: a strong respect for persons in authority, a sense of duty to one's country, an interest and involvement in public affairs.

Jesus taught the acceptance of governmental authority—"Render to Caesar the things that are Caesar's." There is no biblical basis for the civil insolence so recently popular and still in evidence. This is not to say that we should accept everything our political leaders do or approve of every national policy. We may wish to march, demonstrate, or otherwise protest an injustice; but if we keep the proper balance we will be much too busy in *constructive* reform to engage in *destructive* practices.

Helping our children grow up to be good citizens is one of the most valuable contributions we can make to our country.

MANNERLINESS

Good manners grace the Christian's walk, and there is no area that will benefit more from early and consistent home training. Most impoliteness in children is not deliberate maliciousness, but thoughtlessness resulting from a natural self-interest.

Therefore, training, not punishment, should be the emphasis. This should be positive. "It is good manners to . . ." rather than "It is very impolite to . . ." It should be given without nagging, not, "If I've told you once, I've told you a hundred times."

This training will promote in our children a respect for others, particularly their elders, and cultivate a winsomeness that will increase their opportunities for Christian witness.

COURAGE

Heroism on the battlefield or in a scene of high drama captures everyone's imagination, but often overlooked is the day-to-day courage shown by people who stand firmly by their principles. This is the kind of bravery that our children need to learn.

We can help them develop this strength of conviction by capitalizing on their growing desire for independence and resisting the temptation to fight their battles for them. We should give a child all the background support he needs, but let him meet his problems face-to-face.

Each time he successfully defends his personal convictions, his courage is strengthened. He will thus become better prepared to make right decisions despite worldly influences, and to maintain firm beliefs despite opposition.

KINDNESS

Our children need strong home training to counteract the selfish spirit prevailing today that is cold to the needs and interests of others. They need to be shown, by word and example, that the Christian's touchstone is love, which manifests itself in warm, thoughtful action.

Most children are basically kindhearted, but need prompting to show thoughtfulness in practical ways. They need to be alert to opportunities to be kind, such as running errands for shut-ins, writing thank-you notes for gifts, doing volunteer work for a worthy cause. By our example we can teach sympathy and ready forgiveness. Insisting on gentleness to animals is part of this training.

INDUSTRIOUSNESS

In this age of the shorter workweek and the longer coffee break, industriousness is a fading virtue. Children no longer "need" to take a paper route or vacation job—they must be allowed to "relax" after so much pressure at school.

It seems that the religious world is also suffering from this decrease in personal initiative and enthusiasm for hard work. Even Christian homes are sending out pampered, soft young people, unwilling and unable to respond to a call to sacrificial Christian service.

Even in an affluent society when the extra income is not a necessity, a job to give a child training in perseverance and dependability is still desirable. Beginning at an early age, the receipt of an allowance should depend on the faithful accomplishment of assigned household duties. A child should learn by experience that it is necessary to work for what he wants; the world does not owe him a thing. As he becomes older, outside jobs help him develop diligence and responsibility.

Virtuous living is admirable, but it is not an end in itself. What is more important is that the possession of these virtues makes possible a more useful, fruitful life of Christian service.

Chapter 11

Your Child and . . .
Sex Education

"Mommie, Mommie!" Six-year-old Karen burst into the kitchen like an exploding firecracker. "Did you get me with Green Stamps—did you really?" Her eyes were fast filling with tears. "And Jennifer says if you don't like me, you can take me back and get another one."

By now she was sobbing. Her mother stopped washing dishes, dried her hands quickly, and clasped the unhappy little girl tightly to her.

"Why, no, dear. We didn't get you with Green Stamps, or with any other color of stamps. God sent you as a special gift to Mommie and Daddy."

Karen's sobs gradually softened. "And then . . . and then you can't send me back if I am bad."

Mother laughed warmly. "No, it's not just that we *can't* send you back. It's that we wouldn't *want* to anyway."

Karen jumped down from her mother's lap, her eyes now bright through the tears. "I'm going to go and tell Jennifer the real way."

And she was gone in a flash.

The age may vary, the circumstances may never be the same, but there comes a time when you must answer your first question about sex. And no matter how simple it is, there is that initial hesitation, for you know the importance of handling this subject carefully.

These suggestions may help us to provide wise teaching about sex.

The Biblical Plan for Sex Education

Emphasize the sacredness of sex. The home is the best place to give sex its proper importance within the framework of love. It has been only the failure of the home that has forced the introduction of sex education into the schools, where a necessarily detached, scientific program tends to promote an amoral, earthy attitude.

Teach that sex is a God-given blessing, and use biblical principles in your instruction: "Keep thyself pure." "Let no man despise thy youth; but be thou an example . . . in purity." "Your body is the temple of the Holy Ghost."

Dressing a little girl modestly from the first encourages a proper respect for the body. She should be taught always to dress appropriately, whether for church or for a picnic. This guidance should not be just a negative list of "do nots." Peter gives the positive side of true femininity —adornment with "chaste conversation" and "a meek and quiet spirit."

Often the subject of purity is belabored with girls, and then neglected with boys. It is just as important to teach the latter a respect for womanhood and the need for chastity in their own conduct. There is no room for a double standard here—no allowance for a "natural" masculine tendency to "sow wild oats."

71

The Love Example in the Home

Show by example the happiness of deep married love. Basically, a joyous, harmonious atmosphere is maintained in the home when there is a strong mental and verbal communion between husband and wife.

But beyond this, an appropriate display of physical attraction is desirable to give a balanced picture of married life. The husband should not feel embarrassed to kiss his wife good-bye in front of the children, or give her a big bear hug after a specially prepared meal. Children brought up in a home where there is no physical expression of love usually find it very difficult to adjust in their own marriage.

Questions and Answers

Give factual answers to all questions. There is no need for the folklore approach of "baby in the doctor's black bag," even with very young children. If we feel shaky about the proper details to communicate to children, there are many good books on the subject. It is best to call the parts of the body and their functions by their medical terms; slang expressions and nicknames give a flippant air.

Guard against giving more information than is needed or can be understood at any given stage in the child's life.

The story is told of a little boy who came in from play to ask his mother, "Where did I come from?"

She was a very conscientious, modern mother who had thoroughly armed herself for such a question. She set her son down and explained at length the complete story from *A* to *Z*.

After she had finished, her son replied with a flat, "Oh . . . I just wondered. Billy says he came from Cincinnati, and I wondered where we lived before we came here!"

Give a complete enough answer that the child's natural curiosity is satisfied, but don't confuse him with too many unnecessary details. If we aren't sure just how complex an answer to give, some clarifying questions can be asked to determine exactly what the child wants to know.

Usually the information is best given over a long period of time, beginning with simple explanations and gradually going to the more complex queries. This eliminates the need to suggest, "You'd better tell Jimmy the complete story about the birds and bees."

Maintain a relaxed, matter-of-fact attitude in all discussions about sex. If we show embarrassment or uneasiness, the child catches this mood immediately and will become reticent about confiding his questions. The use of a secretive, hushed tone will suggest shame or wrong, and the child may grow up with a crippling sense of guilt in connection with sex.

To supplement what we might tell the child, we should provide reading material appropriate to the child's age level. A Christian bookstore almost always has well-written graded materials giving reliable sex information. This will not take the place of parental guidance, but is valuable as a supplement, and especially helpful with shy children who are hesitant to broach the subject.

Dealing with Specific Sex Practices

Avoid situations when children's sex play may be encouraged. Since boredom is the cause of many problems along this line, it is important to keep children busy, especially with lively activities where natural energy can be expended. Playing behind closed doors should be discouraged. Adequate supervision should be maintained at all times. If we are uncertain of the care provided in other places, we would be wise to encourage our children to bring their friends home to play.

However, it is possible to be so suspicious as to encourage secretiveness, and to be so straitlaced as to promote prudishness. The key here is to be observant without being hovering, to be careful without being overcautious.

If children are found engaging in sex play, do not panic or be shocked. It is a very natural occurrence. It does not stem from "evil minds" but from natural curiosity. Merely break up the activity with a calm, matter-of-fact expression and suggest a new game. Do not lecture or give the impression that the participants have been "bad."

At a later time, we may want to discuss this with our children who are old enough to understand. We could emphasize the wonder of our bodily makeup and discuss its special purposes.

If masturbation becomes evident, show the same understanding attitude and resist the temptation to make it a big issue. Almost all boys, and many girls, practice it for some period during childhood without ill effects. In fact, some Christian advisors view masturbation as a healthy, desirable outlet for a natural, God-given drive. Although others will not encourage this position, most would agree that we should approach this sympathetically and take care not to condemn. It is the guilt feelings produced that have a serious psychological effect—not the practice itself.

FAMILY MODESTY

Rules of modesty for the home will vary for each family, depending on the sex and ages of children and on the parents' background. There is no "right" or "wrong" here; an ideal situation is reached when each family member feels comfortable with the standard.

We may find our children will be inconsistent with their ideas of modesty or even change overnight. One day a pre-teen boy will nonchalantly walk past his parents from the shower with only a carelessly draped towel. The next day he may insist on total privacy just to tuck in his shirt. A five-year-old will suddenly demand a closed bathroom door.

We need to learn to accept these caprices as a normal part of the growing-up process. Children are very sensitive in this area, so it is never kind to ridicule. We should honor new demands of modesty and adjust our family customs gradually as our children grow older, so no one is ever embarrassed.

Whatever our standard, respect for individual privacy should be taught, with *both* adults and children knocking before entering closed doors.

If we have been careful in the early years to give adequate and appropriate sex training, we will have fewer problems in those crucial teen-age years, and our children will have a good chance to become happy, well-adjusted adults.

Chapter 12

Your Child and . . .

Vocational Guidance

Every parent wants his child to grow up to be a success in life. That is natural and right.

But we Christian parents judge success by different criteria from those the world uses. We wish for our children the kind of success that comes only by following God's plan for their lives.

General Guidelines

The child must make a vocational choice for himself. However, there are ways we can guide him in the early years so that it will be easier for him to make the right decisions later.

1. Recognize and accept a child's capabilities. Don't set goals that are beyond his reach.

The Phi Beta Kappa parents may find it difficult when their daughter, even with her best effort, can't get a grade above a *C*. But they must not only resist the temptation to pressure for higher grades but learn to appreciate the conscientious effort she puts forth to achieve even this much. And if this daughter never has a scholastic record that will permit her to go to college, these parents, if wise, will not make her feel inferior. Instead they will help her work at her goal to become an office worker, say.

The most mentally debilitating impression a parent can give is that the child is not "good enough" for his parents. A child must have a strong sense of personal worth in order to grow up to be a well-adjusted adult. He will get that sense of worth only if the parents appreciate his individual capabilities and not demand something more.

2. Respect individual differences. Don't expect a child to follow the interests or career of his father or of older children in the family.

Conflict here comes when the businessman can't understand his son saying, "Dad, I'm just not interested in joining the family firm." Or the teacher being told, "But, Mom, working on cars really turns me on—I *want* to be a mechanic." Or, "Mom and Dad, I don't care if both my brothers went to college—I want to join the navy!"

3. Resist the urge to pressure a child into any choice. He is not a means to work out your early frustrations and unfulfilled desires. Don't insist he go to college just because you never had the chance to. Don't demand his preoccupation with financial security just because your childhood was plagued by poverty.

4. Discuss a wide range of occupational choices. Don't belittle some of the "common" jobs while pushing prestige careers.

5. Remain neutral about childhood decisions. Your budding doctor of one day may decide to be a bulldozer operator the next.

6. Teach self-discipline, which will be an asset in any occupation.

7. Gather information on vocations and seek out trained advisors. Utilize school guidance programs.

As the child grows older, arrange for part-time jobs or

volunteer service in areas of possible interest. For example, the girl who wants to be a nurse can become a candy-striper. Your future businessman can start on the ground floor as a stock boy at the local supermarket.

GUIDELINES FOR CHRISTIAN EMPHASIS

But these are general suggestions. We may wonder how we can give a more Christian emphasis to this subject. Can we specifically encourage a son to be a minister; or a daughter, a missionary? A more knotty question is: *Should* we give this encouragement for full-time Christian service?

Care must be taken in this area, but some specific suggestions may be helpful.

1. Make the strongest petition in the place of prayer, not to the child. No amount of human persuasion can equal the power of praying a child into the harvest field if that is God's will.

2. Saturate the home atmosphere with the blessings of Christian service. Have pastors and evangelists as frequent visitors. Grasp every opportunity to have the children hear returned missionaries, and actively promote missionary work as a family activity.

3. Make Christian service attractive by avoiding a critical attitude toward God's servants. If every Sunday dinner is a recital of the morning sermon's defects, there is more than a faint chance of your son's taking a dim view of becoming a preacher.

4. Show wisdom in dealing with early "calls." Certainly, don't be amused or make light of them. On the other hand, don't emphasize them to the point that the child feels undue bondage in later years.

5. Encourage children to pray about future vocational decisions, and make it a subject of discussion in family

worship. Emphasize that it is a matter of finding the Lord's will, and not just personal choice.

6. Promote independence. An overprotective attitude by a parent makes it very difficult for a child to have the self-confidence to become a missionary (if that is the issue) and endure the hardships that might be involved.

7. Guard against undue pressure. This can produce rebellion not only against Christian service, but against Christ himself. In a more sensitive child this can cause guilt feelings, stemming from an inability to reconcile his own feelings with others' expectations.

8. Make available information on religious institutions of higher education. Bible schools and church colleges provide an atmosphere which often cultivates the young person's desire to give himself to full-time Christian service.

This is not to say that a secular college is an unwise choice. Often, because of a special career choice, it is the only alternative. As discussed in an earlier chapter, the questions of Christian schools versus secular ones must take into consideration many factors. But we should at least see that our young people have adequate information to make the right decisions as to where they will take their advanced schooling.

9. Advocate a Christian approach to a chosen secular occupation. A layman can be a unique witness in areas which are closed to the clergy. If full-time Christian service is not indicated for your child, suggest ways that his secular occupational choice can be used in just as fruitful a manner.

10. Gather up-to-date information to help the child prepare properly for God's service. Most missionaries, for example, are required to have training in a secular field as well as be religiously prepared.

A prospective missionary of today can choose from a

much wider range of occupations than the traditional ones of the ministry, education, and medicine. He can be a pilot, a printer, an agriculturist, a linguist, a builder, an electrical engineer, or a stenographer.

Specialized study can open new avenues of service for the minister in the homeland, too. Marriage counseling, inner-city programs, and religious education are some of the specialized fields now open.

There is less distinction today between purely secular occupations and religious ones. Short-term missionary assignments, lay-involvement programs, and service-oriented vocations give today's Christian a variety of opportunities to serve the Lord in special ways.

Chapter 13

Your Child and . . .
Professional Help

You would not be reading this book if you believed that parents need no help in raising children. But have you ever wondered if you needed professional guidance to help in your family relationships? Does your child have psychological problems that perhaps a specially trained counselor could handle more successfully than you have been able to?

Fortunately, we need no longer feel a social stigma in seeking outside help for such problems. But parents can often delay this because of a conscious or unconscious feeling that this would reflect upon their own abilities. "If we were good parents," they say, "we could cope with this problem." Or perhaps they are afraid that outside involvement would reveal that they are "raising their kids all wrong."

A few Christian parents might even feel that seeking outside help with problems would reflect upon their religious faith. But probably the chief cause for delay is that they do not honestly know if or when it is needed, and they do not know exactly how to go about it.

BASIC FACTS ABOUT MENTAL ILLNESS

A good beginning for any parent is to read several books on both general and child psychology. Bookstores can recommend some nontechnical paperbacks written in an easy-to-understand style. The Christian bookstore can suggest both secular and religious titles that would be helpful.

Read first for general background knowledge. Don't be confused by differences in terminology and philosophy. Our best guard against extreme positions in this field is to have a variety of sources. We will probably never agree completely with any one author, but this situation is desirable, even essential. After wide reading, we will then be able to arrive at a sensible, workable personal philosophy that draws the best and most applicable from many "schools" of thought.

Most authorities will distinguish between two broad classes of mental illness—psychosis and neurosis. There is really much overlapping of symptoms and methods of treatment of the two.

A psychosis is usually described as a severe psychological disorder in which a person loses contact with reality, such as schizophrenia, manic-depressive illness, paranoia. Psychotics usually need hospitalization, heavy medication, supportive psychotherapy, and sometimes electro-convulsive shock treatment.

This is not a common childhood disorder. A psychotic child's erratic and/or bizarre behavior will cause enough problems that the average parent will not take long in determining that medical help is essential. This child will not necessarily act "abnormal" all the time, but may have long periods of unusual behavior. Staring into space, meaningless repetitious activity, a lack of emotional response to either positive or negative circumstances, are symptoms of the problem.

The term neurosis, on the other hand, describes a more common condition, one which allows a person to function in day-to-day activities but causes internal conflicts which keep him mentally uncomfortable. The degree of neurosis in children (as in adults) can vary greatly: from mild, when professional aid may not be needed; to moderate, when some kind of professional help can be very helpful; and finally to severe, when professional treatment is essential.

Even with this basic knowledge, the parent of a "problem child" may still be bewildered. How severe is "severe," or what is the difference between "mild" and "moderate"?

There is no absolute answer, and no two "authorities" would necessarily give the same advice. But two guidelines may be helpful in determining the acuteness of the situation: the degree of severity and the duration of the problem.

DEGREE OF SEVERITY

All children act irrationally at times. They experience jealousy toward their siblings to some degree. They have their assorted share of anxieties, fears, and frustrations. They are alternately aggressive, or withdrawn, or moody. In short, children have the overwhelming capability of acting most of the time "just like children."

But when any "immature" behavior causes *other* more severe problems—whether in the total family relationship or within the child himself—then a parent must consider seeking outside help. This would be the case, for example, when sibling rivalry provokes physical attacks, or when aggression ruins all positive peer relationships, or when withdrawal causes failure in schoolwork.

Duration of Problem Behavior

Another criterion that is helpful in judging problem behavior is duration. When the problem is not only severe, but persists, then there is reason for concern. A poor report card can cause extreme moodiness—but a normal child will soon recover and decide to "try harder next grading period." However, if this moodiness adversely affects the child's schoolwork over a period of months, then the parents have reason to take direct action.

At six a child may "steal" from his mother's purse because he has not yet learned to respect property rights. However, habitual stealing that persists after much training often is a symptom of deep hostility toward authority. Therapy would be recommended in this situation.

Sexual Matters

Sexual matters is a field where the concerned parent may be most uncertain about the line between normal or abnormal behavior.

All normal children show an interest in sexual matters; most masturbate at some time; many often dislike undressing for a medical examination—all these in various degrees at various ages. But applying the twin tests of degree and duration, we can determine the measure of abnormality involved.

A child who is preoccupied with sexual matters over a long period of time, masturbates habitually in private or public, or is extremely self-conscious about his own body, definitely needs professional treatment.

This is one area where delay can be serious, for sexual maladjustment in childhood is one of the most serious barriers to sound mental health in the adult.

SOURCES OF ADVICE

If we feel that our child definitely has problems that need professional attention—or if we think he *might*—what is our first step?

Start with the family doctor. He can check out all physical possibilities that might be responsible for psychological problems. For example, about 5 percent of bedwetting is caused by organic factors. Persistent headaches can be caused by eyestrain or neurological factors rather than tension. Sugar diabetes could be responsible for an exasperating lethargy.

With the older child, the school is the next source of help. A conference with the principal, teacher, or counselor may convince us, for example, that our child is underachieving, not because of seeming laziness, but because of learning difficulties that need special consideration.

In many schools we may request special testing for the child, and the school psychologist can help in determining whether further testing and/or treatment is desirable.

After reading widely about child psychology, talking to the people at the school, and checking with the family doctor, we may decide that we have been overanxious about just normal childish behavior. Then we can adjust our attitude and behavior accordingly to give the help and understanding all children need in going through the "normal" growing-up process.

However, if the educational and medical authorities support our belief that outside help is necessary or at least highly desirable, what is our next step?

The initial advisors may have already recommended a psychiatrist, a psychologist, or mental-health facility. This kind of professional reference is very desirable since it helps guard against the unqualified. Although most people in the field of mental health are highly conscientious, a few unscrupulous ones will take advantage of the fact that there is a shortage of counselors.

If we have not been referred to someone, we can look in the phone book. Mental-health facilities vary greatly depending on the area but they might be listed under Child-Guidance Centers, Mental-Health Clinics, or Family Services.

In choosing a psychologist, psychiatrist, or social worker in private practice, it is wise to check to see if he is listed in the directory of his main professional association: the American Psychological Association, the American Psychiatric Association, or the National Association of Social Workers.

Whether we choose an agency or a private practitioner depends on the individual situation. Agencies often are the less expensive choice, since many have a sliding scale for fees based on the family income. An agency is a good choice when we have no knowledge of private practitioners available or do not know what type would be best. An agency often combines the services of psychologists, psychiatrists, and social workers, who all contribute in their own way to an individual program. This may include individual therapy, group therapy, or a combination of the two.

On the other hand, someone in private practice may give the child a feeling of more individualized attention. And the professional will quickly refer to someone else a client who needs a special kind of therapy that he is not particularly qualified to provide.

The Non-Christian Counselor

Can a non-Christian counselor help the Christian family?

The answer is a resounding "Yes!"

Many Christians fear that a non-Christian counselor is dangerous, that he will try to tear down religious convictions or belittle a fervent faith. Almost all Christian professionals in this field will firmly deny that this will happen. A conscientious counselor does not impose his own values and beliefs on any subject, and that includes religious issues. Only if religion becomes a negative force in a person's search for mental stability would a counselor question his beliefs, and then rightly so. If it is a positive force, most counselors would be quick to appreciate its value to the client's growth, and work from that base.

Christian Counselors

If qualified Christian counseling is available, we should by all means take advantage of it. This will give an added dimension to the treatment, speeding up the improvement. This is especially true with older children and teen-agers whose problems may be mixed in with religious questioning. The Christian counselor may be quicker to recognize the problem and perhaps have even experienced some of the same problems himself. He can establish rapport much more quickly.

However, all Christian counselors would warn us not to expect overnight changes under their guidance any more than we would with a non-Christian. Treating mental illness and emotional problems is a complex job, even with the added dimension of spiritual guidance and prayer. God has not promised the Christian immunity from mental illness and emotional disorders. Although faith in God often sustains a person during these times, God seems to ordain that much help will come through human channels.

THE PARENT'S RESPONSIBILITY

Not all "problem children" will "turn out bad" even if professional counseling is not provided during the childhood years. Humans have an amazing way of adapting, and many adults are adequately coping with problems that developed when they were children. However, childhood problems can develop into more severe problems in the adult. Many people could have been saved much emotional stress (and money) had some of their problems been faced earlier.

The Christian parent has another consideration also. He knows that psychological problems can often limit a person's effectiveness in Christian service. Although Christ can be the Saviour of all, irrespective of mental stability or emotional makeup, and although all have differing gifts of service, a person who has strong personal emotional control can usually be used more fully. He can help others because he does not have to concentrate on his own problems. For example, most mission boards require prospective missionary candidates to go through psychological testing to determine if they can stand the stress of intensive Christian service in the pressure-filled life on the mission field.

Of course, many examples could be given of Christians who have come through mental illness, even a severe affliction, to be creative and victorious. Their ability to relate to and help others is even heightened by the experience. But even most of them would agree that, for the child with psychological problems, professional counseling would be one of the best ways to help him increase his potential to live an abundant Christian life.

Chapter 14

Your Child and . . .
Christian Commitment

Strong family loyalty, high moral standards, sound biblical knowledge—these are goals all Christian parents have for their children. But as admirable as these are, they pale beside what should be the preeminent aspiration—a child's personal commitment to Christ.

THE IMPORTANCE OF INDIVIDUAL DECISION

With religious training in the home considered to be of such influence, why is an individual decision so essential for the child?

1. Secular influences exert a powerful force when a child is no longer totally immersed in his protective home environment. It is quite possible to restrict the actions of our children and, to some degree, dictate their thinking when they are under our control. But when this is no longer possible, only a robust, personal experience with Christ will keep them from being overpowered by opposing influences.

2. Parental influence is limited to the human level. Only God can give the spiritual protection needed against temptation.

90

3. A religious home atmosphere can give a false sense of safety. A child may embrace the rituals and habits of Christianity without experiencing real heart change.

4. The Bible teaches that salvation is an individual matter.

GUIDING TO COMMITMENT

But although our children must accept Christ's gift of salvation voluntarily, we can provide an environment that cultivates their interest in spiritual matters. This will make it much easier for them to make the right choice.

1. Pray continually for the spiritual welfare of the family. Prayer is more powerful than any human effort and will be effective long after parental dominance fades.

2. Show by example the joy of a Christ-centered life. Radiate happiness, and let our service for God be given freely and zestfully. This is especially important in homes where parents are very busy in religious work. Sometimes even good activities become so time-consuming and church responsibilities so binding that a vital, personal, spiritual life is neglected. Thus, some children reject Christ because they equate religion with joyless religious duties.

3. Give spiritual meaning to all religious training. Avoid mere mechanical devices. For example, when requiring scripture memorization, we should discuss and explain the passage first; when teaching tithing, we should emphasize the "cheerful giver" aspect rather than cold percentage. The spirit of the law, rather than the letter, should be the main consideration.

4. Present the claims of Christ to each child individually. No amount of general religious training in the home or faithful church attendance will take the place of our personalized, specific invitation to accept Christ. No exact age for this can be firmly established, because the time of

spiritual awakening in children varies considerably, depending on temperament and environment. But it is wise to take advantage of the very early years, when a child's heart is tender and he is most receptive to the Spirit's call.

After Commitment

After our children make a definite commitment, they need careful guidance and loving understanding in their Christian walk.

1. Guard against expecting an "instant saint." The young convert will develop spiritual maturity in direct proportion to his physical and mental growth. Too advanced requirements will bring discouragement and subsequent abandonment of faith. After all, how many years has it taken us to reach our present spiritual level?

2. Show patience with frequent failings. Stress a continual commitment, teaching the child to seek immediate forgiveness when convicted of wrong. If he is inclined to be a frequent seeker in public services, be cautious in restraining him, for a tender conscience is a precious gift. We might encourage him to take care of many matters of concern in private or family prayers.

3. Refrain from using a Christian experience as a disciplinary weapon of pressure. "Now that you're saved, you can't do thus and so" abets a legalistic attitude. Instead, we should promote prayer and the Scriptures as reliable guides to making proper decisions.

4. Provide individual counseling. Although family worship is the focal point for spiritual training in the home, it is desirable that periodically each child have some time alone with a parent for private discussion and prayer. Bedtime is often a good chance for this. I have known even

large families where the parents have alternated responsibilities, so each child would regularly have "his turn" to receive personal attention and guidance.

5. Use wisdom in introducing the sacraments. Baptism is such a significant one-time experience that it is probably wise to delay arranging this until the child is old enough to appreciate its significance. Unless spiritual maturity is highly developed, the earliest time for meaningful baptism is usually during the teen years.

Partaking of the Lord's Supper is a different matter if for no other reason than that it is held regularly. Because of repeated participation it can gain significance gradually as a child deepens spiritually. If he has made a decision for Christ and has expressed a desire to take Communion, he is usually ready for this sacrament, even at an early age. But during these early years it is important that it be explained and its seriousness stressed before each time of participation.

When children are well adjusted, there is a danger of our becoming complacent. They may be well mannered and well behaved, but it is not enough for them just to be "good"; we must pray that they will be "right."